WITHDRAWN

Johnny Depp

BY DALE-MARIE BRYAN

J-B
DEPP
415-1919

Published by The Child's World®
1980 Lookout Drive • Mankato, MN 56003-1705
800-599-READ • www.childsworld.com

Acknowledgments
The Child's World®: Mary Berendes, Publishing Director
The Design Lab: Cover and interior design
Amnet: Cover and interior production
Red Line Editorial: Editorial direction

Photo credits
Featureflash/Shutterstock Images, cover, 1, 21, 29; Helga Esteb/
Shutterstock Images, 5; Seth Poppel/Yearbook Library, 7, 9;
Mircea Pavel/Shutterstock Images, 11; Andy Z/Shutterstock
Images, 12; Jim Smeal/WireImage/Getty Images, 15; Rhonda
Birndorf/AP Images, 17; Ron Gallela, Ltd./WireImage/Getty
Images, 19; cinemafestival/Shutterstock Images, 23; Steve Beer/
Shutterstock Images, 25; Peter Mountain, Disney/AP Images, 27

Design elements
Sergey Shvedov/iStockphoto

ISBN 9781614732884
LCCN 2012933677

Printed in the United States of America
Mankato, MN
July 2012
PA02128

Table of Contents

CHAPTER 1

Daring to Be Different

Johnny Depp is not afraid to be different. He has played everything from Willy Wonka to Rango, a lizard in the desert. Some actors play the parts that make the most money. Johnny sticks to the parts he likes. "I couldn't do the work for the money," he said.

When Johnny wants to get away from his life as a busy Hollywood star, he likes to paint pictures of people he admires. Among those he has painted are writer Jack Kerouac, singer Bob Dylan, and his kids.

Johnny poses next to his character from the animated movie *Rango*.

CHAPTER 2

Hard Start

John Christopher Depp II was born on June 9, 1963, in Owensboro, Kentucky. He is the youngest of four children. His father worked for the city. His mother was a waitress.

"I was a weird kid," Johnny said. In first grade, he drew pictures of Frankenstein and Dracula. Later he tried to dig a tunnel from the backyard to his bedroom. Another time, he burned his face trying to eat flames.

One of Johnny's first memories was a night in July 1969. Johnny was outside chasing

Johnny used to catch lizards in his backyard in Florida. He tried to train them to sit on his finger.

Johnny (*left*) considered himself different even as a child.

fireflies. Then a neighbor came out and said that men were walking on the moon. "I stayed up all night," Johnny remembered. He was worried that the moon would be injured somehow.

Johnny was very close to his grandfather, whom he called Pawpaw. Pawpaw died when Johnny was seven. It was the first time Johnny had lost someone close to him. The loss was hard for Johnny.

Things got worse soon after when Johnny's family moved to Florida. It took almost a year for Johnny's dad to find a job there. So the whole family had to live in a motel during that time. That was just one of many times Johnny moved growing up. In fact, the family moved more than 30 times before Johnny was 15. Then Johnny's parents got a divorce. "What happened to my family?" Johnny remembers thinking.

Johnny had little interest in school. He was bored there and did not fit in. So he dropped out when he was 16. However, Johnny continued to read and learn on his own.

Johnny had a difficult childhood.

CHAPTER 3

Music First

Johnny's uncle was a **gospel preacher**. Johnny remembers watching his uncle preach. The uncle could grab and hold people's attention with his words. Johnny wanted to do the same thing. The uncle also had a gospel rock band. Johnny watched them play and got hooked.

Johnny's mother bought him his first electric guitar when he was 12. It cost just $25. After that, all he wanted to be was a rock star.

Johnny loved playing his guitar and making music. He listened to records and taught himself to play. He learned how to make the chords from pictures in a book. "[Music is] still my first love," he said.

Soon Johnny and some other kids formed a band. They played at parties in people's backyards. His

Johnny's first love was playing the guitar rather than acting.

band was called Flame. Flame later became the Kids. The band did well in Florida, where Johnny lived. So they tried taking their music to Los Angeles,

Johnny moved to Los Angeles, California, to pursue a music career.

California. However, the band did not catch on very well there.

Johnny had to take other jobs to make ends meet. He even sold personalized pens over the phone. Johnny used different voices on the calls, pretending to be other people. He later said it was good practice for acting.

CHAPTER 4

Reluctant Actor

Johnny loved making music. He was simply not
having much luck at it. One day he met actor Nicolas
Cage. Cage knew of a movie role that did not require
acting experience. It involved a
teenager being eaten by a bed.
Cage introduced Johnny to
his **agent**. Johnny soon quit
the Kids to become an actor.

Johnny's first movie role
was in a horror flick. It was
called *A Nightmare on Elm Street*.
He enjoyed the experience and
decided to continue acting. Johnny had some roles on
television and in a movie called *Private Resort*. The movie
did not do very well, though. Johnny decided he wanted

Johnny got his
first role in a
movie because the
teenage daughter
of the director and
her friend liked
him.

Johnny, shown in 1987, looked to acting when his music career did not take off.

to learn more about acting after that. So he went to classes at a place called the Loft Studio in Los Angeles.

Two years later, Johnny earned a role in *Platoon*. It was a movie about the Vietnam War. That experience taught Johnny how hard acting can be. To prepare, he had to live in the jungle. He had to go through the same training soldiers do. The movie went on to win awards. But most of Johnny's **footage** was cut out. The director thought Johnny was taking attention away from the main character.

Johnny played his guitar in the 2000 movie *Chocolat.* He had to eat a lot of chocolate while filming. Eventually, he started to hate it. However, he later went on to star as Willy Wonka in *Charlie and the Chocolate Factory.*

Losing his scenes was tough for Johnny. But he did not give up. Soon his agent got a call. Somebody who had seen *Platoon* wanted Johnny to act in a television series. Johnny's agent suggested he **audition** for the part. The show was called *21 Jump Street*. It was about undercover police officers. But Johnny had no interest.

The producers still wanted Johnny. Eventually they convinced him to take the part. The show helped

Johnny became famous after his role on *21 Jump Street*. However, he did not enjoy working on that show.

make Johnny a star. But he was not happy being part of it. So he left the show in 1990. He said he would never take a part he did not believe in again.

It can be very hard to find acting jobs. Johnny took a risk by leaving a popular show. But the risk paid off. Johnny got the **lead role** in a 1990 movie called *Cry Baby*. His big break came as part of a popular movie released later that year. Johnny had the lead role in *Edward Scissorhands*. It was about a young man with blades for hands. Because of Johnny's past, he could understand the character's loneliness.

Johnny's next major role came in 1993's popular film *What's Eating Gilbert Grape*. It reminded Johnny of where he used to live. Johnny was still unhappy about his past. Filming the movie helped him feel better.

Johnny is afraid of clowns and spiders. When a friend gave him a tarantula, he had to give it away.

Johnny arrives at the opening for *What's Eating Gilbert Grape* in 1993.

19

CHAPTER 5

Changed Man

Johnny had made some poor choices while growing up. He used illegal drugs and lived a dangerous lifestyle. That continued even after he became an actor. It also continued while he was briefly married in the early 1980s. But his life changed in 1998. That is when he met Vanessa Paradis. She was a singer and actress from France. They became life partners and had two children together. He said having kids changed his outlook on life.

Johnny's two children are named Lily-Rose and Jack. Johnny used to play Barbies with Lily-Rose when she was young.

Johnny's taste in acting roles changed after having kids. He began choosing more

Johnny and Vanessa Paradis began their relationship in 1998.

kid-friendly movies. One example was the Pirates of the Caribbean series. Johnny played the main role of pirate captain Jack Sparrow. Watching cartoons with Lily-Rose helped Johnny prepare for the role.

CHAPTER 6

Awards

Johnny has come a long way since his earliest days as an actor. Many people think he has become one of the best actors in Hollywood. After all, Johnny has won many awards for his acting. The Academy Awards are considered the most important for movie actors. Johnny has been **nominated** for the Academy Award for Best Actor three times. The first time was for *Pirates of the Caribbean: The Curse of the Black Pearl* in 2003. He was up for the award again in 2004 for *Finding Neverland*. Johnny got his third nod for his role in the 2007 film *Sweeney Todd: The Demon Barber of Fleet Street*.

Many adult fans like Johnny for his serious roles. He appeals to many kids, too. Johnny won the Kids'

Johnny's pickiness about his movie roles has paid off with many award nominations.

Choice Awards twice. One was for *Pirates of the Caribbean: At World's End* in 2008. He also won for *Alice in Wonderland* in 2011. Johnny has also been a favorite for Teen Choice awards and MTV movie awards.

The Hollywood Walk of Fame in California features stars that honor some of the biggest names in entertainment. Johnny received a star of his own in 1999.

Johnny's star on the Hollywood Walk of Fame

CHAPTER 7

Giving Back

Johnny has long made an effort to give back to the community. He is most passionate about helping children's **charities**. In fact, he won the Courage to Care award in 2006 for his work with kids.

Pirate captain Jack Sparrow might be Johnny's most famous character. So in January 2008 he dressed as that character. Johnny then paid surprise visits to patients at a children's hospital. He also gave the hospital $2 million.

In 2007, Johnny donated his handprint for a book filled with celebrity handprints. The book was sold to raise money for children's charities.

**Perhaps Johnny's most famous character is
Captain Jack Sparrow from the Pirates of
the Caribbean movies.**

CHAPTER 8

The Future

Johnny has learned a lot about acting over the years. One thing that he finds very important is playing roles that he enjoys. Johnny has already played everything from a pirate to an animated character. Eventually, he said he would like to act in a play by the famous English writer William Shakespeare.

Johnny is also interested in playing historical heroes. He planned to star as Tonto in a Lone Ranger movie in 2012. The Lone Ranger was a western hero in a television show from the 1950s. Tonto was his Native American sidekick.

When not working, Johnny looks forward to being with his family. One of his favorite places to be is on his own private island in the Caribbean. His family spends a lot of time there. The island is one of the few

Johnny wants to continue playing only the roles that interest him.

places Johnny can go and just be himself, just how he likes it. "I can come down here and disappear," he said.

GLOSSARY

agent (AY-junt): An agent manages the business side of an entertainer's career. An agent helps Johnny get roles in movies.

audition (aw-DISH-uhn): An audition is when actors try out for a role in plays or films. Johnny's agent wanted him to audition for a television show.

charities (CHAR-i-tees): Charities are organizations that provide money or assistance to those in need. Johnny has helped children's charities.

footage (FUT-idge): Scenes in a movie are called footage. Some footage of Johnny was cut out of *Platoon*.

gospel preacher (GAHS-pul preech-ur): A gospel preacher is a religious speaker who talks about the newest part of the Christian Bible. Johnny's uncle was a gospel preacher.

lead role (LEAD rohl): The actor who plays the main character has the lead role in a production. Jack Sparrow was the lead role in the Pirates of the Caribbean movies.

nominated (NAH-muh-nate-id): To be named a finalist for an award is to be nominated. Johnny has been nominated for the Best Actor award at the Academy Awards.

FURTHER INFORMATION

BOOKS

Dahl, Roald. *Charlie and the Chocolate Factory*. New York: Knopf, 1964.

Murphy, Maggie. *Johnny Depp*. New York: PowerKids Press, 2011.

WEB SITES

Visit our Web site for links about Johnny Depp: **childsworld.com/links**

Note to Parents, Teachers, and Librarians: We routinely verify our Web links to make sure they are safe and active sites. So encourage your readers to check them out!

INDEX

ABOUT THE AUTHOR

Dale-Marie Bryan is a former elementary teacher and the author of several books for children. She writes from the home she shares with her husband and many pets in southeast Kansas.